EXPRESSIONS
OF
THE HEART

The Second Edition

Written By Angel Moreira

ISBN: 0692899545
ISBN 13: 9780692899540
Angel Moreira Publishing: New York City, New York

CONTENTS

First Expressions
INTRODUCTION OF EXPRESSIONS

Second Expressions
EXPRESSIONS IN RELATIONS

Third Expressions
EXPRESSIONS FOR WOMEN

Final Expressions
EXPRESSIONS OF LOVE A MAN DESIRES

First Expressions:
INTRODUCTION
OF
EXPRESSIONS

Understanding Love

Before you can love,
You have to understand what love is.
And there's no love
Without understanding.

Always learn to love yourself
Before attempting to love someone else.

Take care of yourself
Before you take care of anyone else.

You should be right
Before anyone else enters your life.

And don't misunderstand
The requirements that love demands.

You'll have wonderful times,
But there will also be problems on your hands.
Everything will not always go the way you plan.
You just have to understand—

That's love.

Communication

What good is a train
Without a track?
What good is cereal
Without any milk?

The point I'm trying to prove is that
Communication is needed in a relationship,
And that's a very important fact.

You cannot succeed with love
Without communication.

You can't be faithful
Without showing dedication.

But in order to dedicate,
You have to communicate.

Listen to your mate.
Pay attention; understand his or her feelings.

And don't be afraid to express
How you feel.
Let your partner know everything. Just be real.

Talk to one another.
Don't feel ashamed to cry out to your lover.

Inform your lover on what you are
Facing.
Because when you are in
A relationship, you need
Communication.

Second Expressions:
EXPRESSIONS
IN
RELATIONS

Soul Mate

You are my everything.
And I can't believe we are so close to each another.
I can't believe that we are so cool
With each other as lovers.
We're like sister and brother.

Like the birds and the
Bees,
Like trees need leaves,
Like Adam needed Eve.

That's how I need you
And you need me.

We have that emotional
Connection,
That strong bond,
And you have that love that's the
Bomb.

We are two of a kind.
You are the other me.

My soul mate,
My love,
And my destiny.

Marriage Material

Someone who's beautiful
Inside and out,
From the outer
To the inner soul.
Someone who loves you through
The smooth and rocky roads.

Someone with a good
Heart,
Without any intention of breaking you
Apart.

Someone who has
Integrity and
Understands life and
Spirituality.
A soul that really makes you
Happy.

Someone with a good personality
And a good head on their shoulder
And who plans for the future as
You get older.

Someone who respects you,
Protects you.
And someone who will never
Forget you.
Someone you are compatible with,
Like soil that needs minerals—
That's someone who's marriage material.

Love Doesn't Have A Complexion

True enough,
We are from different cultures, religions,
And backgrounds.
But I still love having you
Around.

I don't care about the differences in our
Hair texture and eyes.
I just want you in my life.

Who cares if your hair is straight
Or nappy?
The only important thing is that you
Make me happy.

Whether your skin is dark or
Light
Is not the determining factor to having
You in my life.

Our hands feel the same as everyone else's,
And you have the same kind of loving.

Our lips are the same,
And those who criticize us for kissing are lame.
It's such a shame
That we have to go through
These things.

But despite it all, I need your kisses
And affection,
And your love doesn't have a
Complexion.

Will You Be My Valentine

Will you
Be
The one to share this special day
With me?

A day that represents
Loving and sharing,
Giving and caring,
Commitment, dedication, and
Togetherness.

A day that represents
So much joy and happiness.

A day
That lovers love.
A day that determines
What you're made of.

A day
Where you let your love free,
Express everything you feel internally,
And assert your passion
Emotionally.

Do you want to be with me on this day that's
Such a test in time?
Will you be with me on this day we call
Valentine's?

Will you be my valentine?

Will You Marry Me

I remember when
I loved having fun,
Way back then—

Before real love
Began,
Before my bachelor days came to
A end.

Before I met you
And reformed.
Before this new man was
Born.

I used to play,
Play so many games,
And break,
Break so many hearts.
I never understood why anyone
Would love me from the start.

Now my mind that was once corrupted
Is pure.
And your love, I have endured.

You are the only
Woman I see.
Who else in this world can
Put up with me?

This is why I must ask
As I get on one knee,
"Will you marry me?"

Sucker For Love

Sucker for love,
Sucker for love,
Sucker for love.

You're a sucker for love.

You're doing things
You never thought you would do
Because love has a hold on you.

You are breaking and bending
Your back,
Conducting yourself with peculiar
Acts,

Going out of your
Way
In every way,
Just to make someone else
Happy.

And sometimes you give what you don't
Necessarily have,
Just to make the feeling last.

Oh, man,
You no longer hang with your friends.

You are a sucker for love.

But it's OK.
You could be a sucker for love—
That's true.
Just make sure that the other individual is a sucker for you too.

12

What She Got On Me

You've been creeping,
Freaking,
And sleeping around on me.

I decided to follow my intuition,
So I followed you around, and guess
What I see?

Wow!
You could have at least found someone
Who looked better than me.

You went from first class
To street booty.

I mean...

Look at her:
"That's ugly."

This is who you were with when you didn't
Call me
This is what you've been hanging out with in
The streets?

But you're going to be sorry, sorry, sorry.

Because there will never be another love like me.
(Take a deep breath)
I'm not going to cry about it or grieve,
Because she doesn't have anything on me.

PS: Just because a man has eyes to see, that doesn't mean he's not
blind.

The Churchgoer With The Street Lover

You know, you know, you know—
You know
That you and your partner have to be equally
Yoked.

How will this work?
They are in the streets,
And you are at church.

When you want to pray,
Someone wants to play.

You take God serious,
And they just act curious.

They've told you that Sunday morning
They will show.
But for some frivolous reason, someone did not
Go.

How long can this last?

Will they ever see the picture?
Will they ever deliver?

When will they walk the walk of
Faith?
Will they ever see life God's way?

You Feel So Good

I'm on top of you,
Looking upon your face,
And the sensation feels so great.

As you whisper in my
Ear,
Holding me tightly,
Breathing heavily,
While you softly moan, telling me to take you
There.

I'm grinding and working,
Hoping you're getting close,
Because I want you to explode.

Your body smells so sweet,
And I'm praising it as if it
Was a temple,
Enjoying the feeling as I ride
In you.

I know you feel it because
You're beginning to shake and your eyes are squinting.
It's about to be over any minute.

And I want to finish with a kiss as I look at you,
Face-to-face,
While telling you that you feel so great.

Let's Take It Slow

We've been dating for a
Couple of months.
I've been patiently waiting for you,
And now you think it's time
To give me your love.

I'm going to take it nice and slow,
Not fast and furious
Or fierce and vigorous.

The lights are low,
And I'm ready to get you in
The mood.
I know this is something you're not
Used to.
However, don't worry because I will be
Gentle

As I kiss you,
Right there
And right here.

Now let me nibble a little on
Your ear.

I'm ready to give you a nice warm-up
Game,
And after this you will never be the same.
You've been waiting for years for someone
Who cares.
Now I'm here,
So let go
As I take my time with your body
And give it to you nice and slow.

It's Your Night

Baby, it's your night.
The candles are lit.
Your dinner is fixed.

And after you walk in the
Bedroom doors,
I'm all yours.

I'm your love slave.
It's what you say.

So follow the rose petals to
The room.
Wait—
Let me take another look at
You.

At times I feel like I'm
Dreaming
When I'm inside you.

I have some toys
And tools:
Handcuffs, ropes, and some ice to stay
Cool.

Pick what you want to
Use because it's your night,
And I'm here to make you feel
Real nice.

I'm Falling In Love With You

I feel like I'm in this
Great dream,
Deep in my
Sleep,
As something comes inside
Me.

I'm afraid to awake
Because this wonderful feeling will
Fade.
And my heart, you'll take.
But in reality my eyes are wide open,
And it's faith.

It's so unbelievable
That my smile is as wide
As a football field.
I have to consistently tell myself
That this is real.

And I can't slim down my smile.
I'm like a child
On the playground

Because of you.
And now
I'm falling, falling, falling, falling—
I'm falling in love with you.

I'm In Love With The Thought Of Loving You

I don't know you
Yes, that's true.

You could be insane or
Crazy,
But I can see us getting married.
I can see you having my baby.

You may have many characteristics I
Hate,
But I still think I would want to wake up every
Morning to see your face,
While serving you breakfast on your plate.

I don't know.
I just feel something for you in my heart.

Something that's telling me
Love has found me.

Or maybe it's just a fantasy
That will never come true.
Or maybe I'm just in love with
The thought of being in love with you.

Just The Thought Of You
Makes Me Smile

It could be in the middle of the
Day,
And I just get into this
Daze,
Thinking about your smile, your pretty eyes,
And your ways.

You are just so incredible,
With a personality that's
Unforgettable
And a body that's
Delectable.

Sometimes I feel you're
Too good for me
Because you are just so
Lovely.

Sometimes I feel that you falling for me is
A mistake.
But I'm glad you are here because I'm so
happy you came my way.

I haven't felt this good in such
A while,
And the thought of you just makes me smile.

Dangerously In Love

It's kind of scary how much
I love you.
It's not normal to need someone the
Way I need you.

It's hazardous to be addicted to
Someone
The way I'm addicted to
You.

And what they say is
True:
Too much of anything is not good
For you.

Even though I can't get enough of you,

I love the way you smell.
I love the way you taste.
I love the way you kiss.

Who would have ever thought I could
Feel like this?

But I do.
I feel as if I'm too
Into you,
And I'm dangerously in love with you.

Baby-Mama Drama Part I

I've been seeing you for sometime
Now,
And I like you.
I think you are cool,
And we share times that are memorable.

Then suddenly the phone
Rings,
And it's the mother of your child
Calling.

"It's really late.
Do you know what time it is?"
This leads me to question.

We could be having a good
Time.
Then guess who
Arrives?

We can't do anything without her
Popping up.

Then, when I call you to see where
You are,
You are with your baby's
Mother.

She's always causing chaos.
I wish she would get lost.

And when I want to enjoy your
Company,
You are somewhere looking for her
So that you can give her some money.

She's always showing her face
She needs another man.
That's all I have to say.
I really don't need all this drama
And all these unnecessary conflicts
With your baby's mama.

Baby-Mama Drama Part II

You said that I was
Sorry
And that you didn't
Need me.

So now I'm with someone else
And happy,
So stop calling me.

You informed me that you would
Be better off by yourself and you
Could hold down the fort.
Then I get a call saying that I have to
Pay child support.

Stop calling
My family,
Asking about me.
It's not my fault that you put yourself
In misery.

I know your mission is to destroy everything
I have going for me,
Even if you have to use
The baby.

I never thought that you
Could be so crazy,
And I understand that it's hard to
Get over me.
But you can:
This world is filled with other
Men.

Baby-Father Drama

I don't want you.
I don't want you.
I don't want you.

So stop stressing me and
Threatening me,
Telling me what you are going to do to
The next guy I see.

Stop stalking me.

You didn't know what to do with me
When I was yours.
You should have known that me leaving you was a
Loss.

But I guess you don't know what you got
Until it's gone.

Gone,
Gone,
Gone.

Because you treated me so
Wrong.

Wrong,
Wrong,
Wrong.

Let it go,
Because I don't want you anymore.

You should have tried to love me
Right a little harder.

Because now I will only perceive you as
My baby's father.

It's Your Loss

You're too this.
You're too that.

You point out every
Negative trait
And comment that I'll never
Have anyone this way.
But you never acknowledge the
Positive things I bring.

It's like you don't take
The time
To explore what's in my heart and
Mind.

You didn't get to see
The depth in my heart and soul.
But I guess by now you
Are on your own.

You left me alone,
Alone in this world,
Which directed me right to
Another girl.

You left a heart that was made
Of gold.
You didn't want to wait
Around until the gems unfold.
But by now
You will never know.

And someone else will
See
All the wonderful things
Embedded in me.

27

And from what cost
From you being ungrateful
And it's your loss.

Neglected

When I want to smile in
Your face,
You always push me
Away.

When I want to have you
Around,
You have to leave
Town.

You don't enjoy
Me,
Or is everything about
Your money?

Because sometimes you get
Caught up in a world of
Your own
As if you are all
Alone,
And you don't realize that there's
Someone in your life.

Sometimes you can be
So stingy,
And then you don't see what you
Are doing to me.

I just wish that you can stop being
So selfish and stop neglecting me.

The Tables Turned

You used to always call me,
But I never wanted to answer.

Over and over, you would ask for
My company,
But I would just tell you that I
Have to do something.

Then you would say
You're never going to have a woman
This way,
But I never thought I would experience it
This day.

I never imagined
The day
I'd check my caller ID
And don't see your name.

I never thought it would
Be a day
A day your feelings would
Change.

And now I want
To call you.
I want to see what you've been
Up to.
But this lesson I've
Learned
And the tables turned.

Get Well Soon

It hurts me deeply to see
You lying in pain.
It causes my eyes to tear
Like rain.

And my brain
Is going insane,

Knowing that you
Are suffering
Day to day,
Recovering.

But you will be
All right.
Tragedy and pain is a part
Of life.

You are going to make it
Through,
And this whole time
I'm going to be right beside
You.

Supporting you,
Holding you,
Loving you,

Doing all I can
Praying and hoping that you
Get well soon.

Only If I Could

Only if I could
Confess,

Only if I could
Let these feelings undress,

Only if I wasn't
So shy,
Then I might have a chance with
Having you in my life.

Only if I could
Be a little more aggressive.

Only if I could stop obsessing.

Only if I could
Take a stand.
But will I rise or start
Falling?

Only if I could
Tell you how I really feel.
One day I will.
Until then, I wish I could tell you what's real.

PS: Crushes can come true, or they can remain a fantasy for you.

Intimidated

Watching you is
So entertaining,
And at times
You have me fainting.

You are so sharp
And always on point,
So appealing, and you make me
High like a joint.

But you are a little
Too much for me,
Mentally, physically, and professionally.

How can I make someone like
You happy?
You seem as if you have everything
You need in your life,
Which excludes me.

I want you so
Bad,
But someone like you I feel I can never
Have.

You are like the major
League,
And I'm the minor league.
And I can't imagine you being in
Love with me.

Only if our statues
Could be traded,
Then I just might not be so intimidated.

From Nothing To Something

I remember the days
We didn't have a thing.
We only had love,
But that seemed to be enough—

The days we lived
With a little change,
But what was inside for you and I remained the
Same.

The times we went
Without having,
Knowing that it would not be
Forever lasting.

The times you didn't
Get much for Christmas,
But you just dealt with
It.

The times when I couldn't
Get what you wanted for Valentine's.

But I still was your only
Focus.
I remember those moments.

We have come a long
Way,
And the sun shines a lot
Brighter today.

The world is
Yours.
We did it, and it was all
For my favorite girl.

We are living life
In luxury
And are not stressed about
Anything.

We have a wonderful place
To live and
College money for the
Kids.

We are winning.
It's a new beginning.

But what I respect the
Most
Is that you gave me all
Hope.
I was rich with love,
And we went
From having nothing
To having something.

Low Finance And Romance

I understand that you love cruises
And diamonds,
Fur coats, and trips to
The islands.

I think everyone would love
To visit an exotic place.
But I think a card with a poem on it
Should put the same smile on your face.

And I know you like to go to
Fancy restaurants most of the time.
I think a nice home-cooked lasagna dish
With candles lit would do just fine,

With a nice bottle of
Red wine
And a nice massage before
Bedtime—

And a little something else
To ease your mind.

Baby, basically, I'm trying to
Get you to understand:
I might be low on finance
But I still can show you romance.

Unleash My Pride

I was wrong, and I
Know it.
But baby it was my ego
That wouldn't let me grow.
It takes all control over me, honestly.

I have to be
Tough.
I have to be
Rough.
I have to make you feel like I
Don't need your love.

Then my ego will
Be pleased,
But inside I'm really
In need.

It's foolish.
I need to be happy,
So I'm telling you
I was wrong,
And I'm sorry.

I let my pride get in
The way,
But I realize I need to make
A change.

Why Break Up Just To
Make Up

Just because we have a little
Argument and fight,
That doesn't mean we should
Be out of each other's life.

Why?

Why let you go
When I know
It's only going to hurt us so?

What are we trying to
Prove?
When you love me and
I love you
And I know you don't want to
Live without me
And I don't want to live without you,
So what's the use?

It's a waste of time
And stress that we don't need on our minds.

Let's just be
Realistic.
We will have
Arguments.
We will not agree on everything.

But we can always resolve
The issue, even when it seems
Like it's too much,
Because it's foolish to break up
Just to make up.

Makeup Sex

It's so annoying:
The conflicts,
The restrictions,
And the distance
Between you and I.

The yelling,
The cursing,
The blaming,
Running game,
And finger-pointing.

Let's put an end to it.
Let's give it a rest.
As you undress
I want to feel some happiness,
To relieve stress.

Give me your joy.
I enjoy
While we make noise and
The neighbors are annoyed.

This is a relief.
I'm reaching my peak,
And it was so beautiful.
Baby, I don't want anyone else
But you.

Let Me Love You Where The
Sun Doesn't Shine

I know you had a
Long day; you look so tense.
Just sit back, relax, and let me
Fix this.

Because I want to cater to my
Beautiful woman.

You feel that?

How about this?
I love the taste of your
Lips.
Now keep them apart as I gently
Lick.

You taste so good.
While you place your hands on my head,
I hope I'm making you feel good.

Because I want you to feel
The way a woman should,
I want to make everything better for you.
I hope this is relaxing you.

As I lick up, down,
Round and round,
Side to side,
Where the sun doesn't shine—
Just tell me when it's time.

Let's Start As Friends

If we start out as
Friends,
I feel we can build a
Better foundation.

I feel that we can
Have a better understanding
Of each other's requirements and
Demands.

I would understand
You,
And you would fully understand
Me.
And we should be able to
Handle anything
So that we do not destroy the
Wedding ring.

But don't feel as if I'm not into
You.
I just want to take my time
So I can know everything about you.

I truly want to be by
Your side
All the way to the end.
I just think it would be better
If we start as friends.

Listening To Your Friends

Why, when you are interested in
Someone
But yet confused,

Do you ask your friends,
"What should I do?"

Do you really think that
They give advice that's helpful?

At times the advice is good,
But sometimes it's not right.

Think about those friends who
Give you negative advice,
But yet they never have anyone
In their life—
Or if they're involved, it's with
Someone not worth talking about.
Then you have those friends who
Do have a good insight.

Therefore, you could miss out
On something because of your
Friends.
Or you could end up having someone
Special because of your friends.

But in the end,
You could listen to your friends—
Meaning, listen to what they have to
Say.

But you should make the best decision
For you at the end of the day.

Thank You

Thank you
For coming into my life.

Thank you
For showing me the light.

Thank you
For completing me.

Thank you
For supporting me.

Thank you
For believing in me.

Thank you
For everything you've done for me.

You make me feel
Incredible,
And I just want to thank
You.

Thank you.
Thank you.
Thank you.

And I love you.

The Chameleon

I thought you were
Someone to respect,
Someone with self-worth,
But your colors changed,
And the truth hurts.

You appeared to be one of the
Sweet ones,
But I guess I was
Dumb.

I thought you were more like the
Suburbs,
But you are more like the
Slums.

You tried to give me a perception
Of you that's healthy and full of wealth,
But in reality you are sick
And full of filth.

And it's so sad
That you are such trash.

How long did you think this
Lie would last?

Were you going to admit
That you are so ridiculous?
The only thing I wish
Is that I hadn't discovered the real you
Like this.

And now when it comes to you.

My hands I wash
Because I see through your camouflage.

PS: Words can only be proven by actions.

I'm So Through With You

Why is that
The more I want to give you
My heart,
The more you want me to
Depart?

All I want to
Do
Is be good to you.

But no,
You choose for me to leave
You.

Then you complain about
Not having a good woman.
But when I'm in your hands,

You fail to fulfill
Certain demands.

Everything I wanted to do
For you,
You preferred something else
For you.

Just to see
How far you can go,
Just to see
If I would fold.

But what you do will fall back on
You,
And now I'm so through with you!

Not Compatible

They say
That opposites attract,
But in this scenario
Love will not work like
That.

I'm very optimistic;
You are very pessimistic.

You are wild and cunning;
I'm innocent.

You love to play around and
Have fun;
I'm always serious trying to get the
Job done.

On Saturday nights you like to
Go to the club;
I prefer to get some rest so in the morning,
While at church, I can show God some love.

You and I
Are kinda like eating breakfast
At night,

Which is not right—
We are not compatible.

Heartbreak

It's like chopping fruit
In a blender
Or trying to get reception
From a television without cable or an antenna.

It's unclear.
It can have you so
Confused,
And the only thing you can wonder is
Why is this happening to you.

What did I do?

To feel this way,
What did I do?
Life is not the same.

And all you wanted
To do
Is love someone who you thought
Was special.

Now your heart
Doesn't have a beat.
You can't feel your
Feet.

You're losing or
Gaining weight.
You look sad in the face.

But during this phase
Stay strong doing the process of mourning.
And know that life goes on, and you are
Only heartbroken.

PS: What one will not do, someone else would love to do.

Unloved

I look to my left, and I see
Love.
I look to my right, and I see
Love.
Then I look at myself,
And realize I need help.

Am I emotionally conflicted
or to loneliness am I addicted?

My heart has been
Suffering
For such a long time
When will I find someone I
Can call mine?

It's not fair.
I can't find love anywhere.

Or does the Lord have someone
Designed only for me
And soon we will meet?

Until then
I guess I'll just keep on moving
And feeling unloved.

Fall Back

You are putting in all the
Effort and all the work.
You make all the phone calls.

But you're not getting a call
Back at all.

Every time you see one another,
It's by your invitation.
That's the only way you two have
Any engagements.

It's supposed to be a two-
Party thing,
But you are doing everything.

Over and over and over.

If you are facing this
Situation,
You might have to fall
Back.

And according to what
That individual do,
Those actions will tell you if that someone
Is really into you.

PS: You can't read a book as one, if you are on two different pages.

Temptation

I've been with the one I love for
A while,
And the relationship is strong.

Everything is going well,
But for how long?

How can I resist
What's evident?
It's obvious
That the opposite sex finds
Me attractive in my residence.

They want to know where my
Head rests at night.
They want to know if my lovemaking
Is right.

They want to know if I'm
A freak and
How I get down in the
Sheets.

And they don't care if I have
Someone in my life with me.

I usually tell them I'm
Sorry
I'm involved and in love
Deeply.

But it's this one individual
Who causes me hesitation.
It's one individual who brings
About so much temptation.

You Opened My Heart

I used to hate the thought
Of love:
Two people always under
Each other.

And happy

That never really
Happened to me.
My mates seem to always
Manipulate, lie, and disappear on me.

Basically loved seemed
Phony.

What was it really
Worth?
Always getting hurt
And constantly treating someone like
Dirt.

But something about you seemed
True.
Also, I don't want to let go
Of you.

You are not the kind to just
Give away,
So I don't want you to go.
I want you to stay.

I knew it was something special
About you from the start.
I guess I was right because you
Opened my heart.

I Really Do Love You

Sometimes you feel like I'm
Lying to you.
When I tell you I love
You,
I always go out of my
Way for you.

But you still question the
Truth.

You're always telling
Me,
"You don't love me."

Do you think the things I do
For you are for nothing?

I feel love when I look into
Your eyes.

And I don't know how you can
Feel otherwise.
It hurts me, so do not
Deny.

At times, it causes me to
Feel miserable.
Don't you know that you
Are irreplaceable?

You come first, and there's not a
Love above you.
And I really, really do love you.

Nothing Is Going to Break Us Up

I may be appealing, and it causes
Many attractions.
But your love is my only
Satisfaction.

I can be charming and
Endearing.
But your heartbeat is what
I'm hearing.

So give me that trust
Because nothing is going to break
Us up.

All the money, excelling, and achievements
I go through
Doesn't lead me to want to leave
You.

Why would you think that I will find
Someone better?
My heart is with you, and I prefer for us to be
Together.

Sometimes I get extremely busy.
And it may cause us to be a little distant,
But I'm still thinking of you every minute.

You say that I can't be trusted,
But I didn't do nothing.

I'm always loyal to you.

Occasionally I may lust,
But you are just

Too much to let go and
Nothing is going to break us up.

Your Parents Don't Like Me

Every time I'm around your
Parents.
I feel uncomfortable.

They never show any
Hospitality
Like it's something wrong
With me.

I understand that it's their
Responsibility to protect their baby,
But this is crazy.

I see the stares.
I see them whispering in one
Another's ear.

Do they think I'm not good
Enough?
Do they feel that I don't deserve
Your love?

Do they feel like you can do
Better?
Do they think that I don't have it
Together?

It's not hard to see
That your parents don't like me.

Psycho Lover

When we started out, you seemed
So normal
I didn't detect that you had
Psychological issues.

A led to B;
B led to C.

But at D, you said I started
To act funny, and I wanted to leave.
Then you became crazy.

I've seen signs,
But you're really losing your mind.

You're like a stalker,
Nightwalker,
Excessive phone caller, day creeper
Grim Reaper.

You're just off, lost, and you can't
Control me. I'm the boss.

I'm caught up in a real-life
Fatal attraction.
Don't make me get an order
Protection.

This is a mess
And a life lesson.

How did I get into this?
Only if I had one wish
I would wish things were different.

PS: There's a love for every love, you deserve better.

I Want More And More And More

We just finished
Our first session,
And it felt as if I was in
Heaven.

We are both worn down and
Sweating.

But it's still early. It's only
Fifteen minutes after eleven.

Let's go all night
Until there's sunlight.

Let's explore one another's
Bodies
As I kiss you
Gently.

Let the love and passion
Free
As I please you and you please
Me.

I'm here open-minded,
So speak.

Let's communicate so
We can really connect
And enjoy the final hours
Of wonderful sex.

Because I want more and more and more.

So Addictive

Hey, what else can I say?
You are incredible at what you do.
Your loving is great.

After you gave that thing to
Me,
I was hooked, and I wanted it
Repetitively.

Do you have a special
Remedy?
Because you got me.

Did you go to school to learn
Special tricks?
Because I never felt anything
Like this.

Now the only thing I can
Do is think of it.
I have to have it.
I need it.

It's my fix,
My secret prescription.
The description is like my
Medicine from heaven.

And I just have to feel
It.
Oh, it's so addictive.

All Over You

I just want to be
All over you.

I can't wait to see you
So I can be all over you.

I love being all over you
While you do what you do.
Move how you move.

I can't help myself.
I have to be all over you.

You Are Always on My Mind

All day,
All night,
You are on my mind.

Summer, winter,
Spring, and fall,
I want to give you my all.

When it's cold
You are my warmth.

When is hot
You are my chill spot.

You have a place
With me.
Mentally and spiritually,
You are what anyone
Would need, baby.

My thoughts
Are lost.
Because of you
I don't feel normal,
Because when people's minds
Are of the world,
I'm thinking of you.

And I'm not sure if there will be a
Time
That you diminish
From my mind,
Because you are always on my mind.

Denial

Why do
I deny,
Deny what's true?

Why do
I deny
When I know I'm head over heels for
You?

Why do
I
Try to run and hide
When I know I want you?

Why do
I
Do the foolish things I do?

Why do
I
Try to act uninterested
When I know I really want it?

Why do I
Deny,
Deny your face,
When I know
Every day
I'm on your social-media page?

I want to really get to
Know you,
But instead I deny you.

How Could I

At times I ask myself
How could
I
Hurt the one I love so much?

How could
I do this?
Did I have to fall for another woman's
Touch?

How could
I
Look at those eyes?

How could
I
Tell all those lies?

I know I should have not done this,
But I'm guilty, not innocent.

How could
I
I know I'm only human
But my love, I don't want to ruin.

What was I thinking?
What was I doing?

Now this is something I have to
Live with.
I know this is not the way you accept God's gifts.

How could I?

Trophy Contract

A trophy—a woman who walks into a room and everything stops; when you look at her, your mouth drops. At any point, she can cause an accident, and she's highly desired by many, many, many men.

If you are involved with a trophy, here are a few rules and regulations for you.

1. If the price is not right, it's on her to decide if you will be a part of her life.
2. Enjoy every second, every minute, and every moment you have because at any point it can end; trophies don't always last.
3. If you were to fall or if your money starts looking funny, you may lose your trophy.
4. Expect different mood switches; trophies are usually narcissistic.
5. She has to look real good, so you have to keep up with her maintenance.
   So keep a steady cash flow, and keep up with your credit-card payments.
6. If there's another man with more credibility than you, she will feel she has the right to leave you.
7. She will never love you more than she loves herself. But if she does and if she's sweet and wants to give to you, while simultaneously breaking the trophy rules, then your search for finding a love should be over and through.

I _____ understand the terms and agree to follow the rules and regulations in the contract that's provided. I will hold myself accountable to my trophy contract.

Name_____
Date_____

Time Invested Wasted

We've been together for some time
Now.
But when I ask you certain questions
You reply, "I don't know."

I'm ready to take things
To the next level,
But it seems like you are digging our relationship
Into a hole with a shovel.

I told you so many times
What I wanted from you,
But you never seem to follow
Through.

I want you to be with me
Fully.

It's like you have one foot in
And one foot out.
With you I will never win.

But what you don't understand
Is that I'm still going to have someone.
And if I can't be with you, someone will
See that I'm special.

What's the problem?
Who are you?

You're going through these phases,
Showing different faces.
I just wonder if my time is
Being wasted.

Let's Wait Awhile

Don't misinterpret anything. I'm attracted to you
Sexually.
But before we intertwine I want to get to know you
Mentally.
I want to know what makes you
Smile.
I want to know what makes you
Cry.
See, I want to know you as an
Individual.
Before I go between your
Tights,
I want to know what's on your
Mind.
What're your future aspirations
In several years of time?
Do you like candy?
Do you like movies?

Do you prefer a bubble bath
Or relaxation in a Jacuzzi?

What's your favorite food?
And when you are stressed, what do you
Normally do?
And how can I be a good asset to you?

Do you enjoy breakfast
In bed?
Or do you rather eat at the table
Instead?

Do you like to cuddle
By the fireplace
Or go camping in the
Woods?

Tell me what you love and hate.
Basically what I'm trying to
Say
Is that I want to make love to you,
But we can wait because I'd rather love you in every way.

I Can't Do It

Yes, you think I'm
Sexy.
And you want to climb all over
Me.
And you want to put it on me.

Despite the fact that I already
Have a girl,
You still want to rock my
World.

And you really don't care
About the love my girl and I share.
You just feel the sexual chemistry in
The air.

I'm sorry.
But I have to deny your invitation
Because my girl is so amazing.

She's too good to
Me,
So why would I want to
Cheat?

But I don't want to destroy
Your confidence.
I just can't do it
Even though you are beautiful and sexy.

PS: If you take care of a good man in every way, he should feel this
way every day.

Third Expressions:
EXPRESSIONS
FOR
WOMEN

The Strength Of A Woman

You are the most dominating force of this
World.
Think about it. A man really doesn't know who
He is until he finds a girl.

You are that missing link
That holds everything together.
Really evaluate your abilities to make
A household better.

And I'm not stating this to seek approval from
You.
I'm saying this because it's true.
What would a man really be without you?

Could a man be able to conceive a
Baby?
Would he have the strength to carry a
Child daily?

Do you think a man could live without
Your touch?
The power of your souls we yearn for
So much.

You are the strongest element God could
Ever make in this world.
That's why I have to respect and acknowledge you
Being a man in this world.

Do you think a man could handle your
Daily tasks?
If a man were a woman, how long do you think
He would really last?

I question if a man can be held accountable for certain
Duties.
However, I'm not saying men are weak.
But a man needs a woman to become what
He needs to be.

And it has been stated that it's a man's
World.
But the strength of a woman is what a man
Needs.

The Greatest Woman

Being with you is like winning the
Lotto.
I feel like I've hit the
Jackpot.
And I've gotten three cherries
On slots.

You know how you see
Flashing lights on the machine?
That's the way my eyes light up
When you step on the scenes.

And you've proven to be the
Best one for me,
My friend to the end and my trophy,
Someone I can take out for show,
Someone who sparkles like
Diamonds,
Someone with a heart made of gold,
Someone who came in my life with
The perfect timing,
Someone who's kind and electrifying,
The one I want to be with until my
Day of dying
And crying going through struggles
While trying.

Someone there during my rises
And falls
Through the beginnings and ends.
But with you, I know I will always win
Because no matter the circumstance,
I would always have the greatest woman.

How To Determine A Man's Riches

I know when you look for a man, you
Look for someone with money.
But love should not correspond with
Money.

The love you have for a man should
Not be determined by
What's in a man's pocket
Or his possessions.

However, here are some key factors to
Consider.

It's not necessarily about what the man drives.
It's about the drive inside him
And his optimistic attitude to win.

It's not about the diamonds he wears around
His neck. Check his assets,
And even if he has a fancy ride and
Nice clothes,

Those liabilities can put him in
Serious debt.
He's acquiring intriguing things so you can
Be impressed.

You may think that your man has money,
But he may not have anything.

Except for a stack of bills.

If you really want a rich man,
You have to find someone who's rich
In mind.

Check his assets, check his assets, check his assets.

Even if he's struggling.
Because to acquire wealth you have to know
How to get it mentally.
Then the cash will appear vividly.

Once his income from his assets surpasses
His monthly expenses from his liabilities,
That's when he can become financially free.

PS: Check his assets and not his liabilities.

Who's The Bigger Player

For so many years and so many
Days,
You've accepted men's ways with the
Games they've played.

All the swears and promises
That've been broken
It seems as if men were always
Joking.

For so many nights, you've
Cried
While trying to be the best woman by a man's
Side.

But now...

The tables have turned,
And it's time for men to burn.

You are fed up with their ways,
And someone has to pay.

And the truth is
You can be effective.

Because in this case women are smarter.
You think before you move
With the things you do.

Men think with the wrong head,
And you play the game like chess.

You analyze,
Then strategize,
Take actions, and then hide.

You hide all your dirt
So that it never appears on earth.

Think about the actions of cats
And dogs.

Let's say the man is a
Dog.
Dogs leave their mess all over the place.

But a cat's more like a woman.
Goes to a private place, does what she has
To do, and then cleans everything up with
Kitty litter.

This is why nowadays so many men are
Bitter.

But the man
Is the veteran
With more experience.

So who's really better?
Who really have their game more together?
Men or women?

Final Expressions:
EXPRESSIONS
OF
LOVE A MAN DESIRES

Loyalty

All men want from you is your
Support.

He wants to know that you will
Always be there.
He wants to know that you honestly
Care.

When the wall falls
And the bricks break,

He wants you to look at him
And smile at him the same way.

Don't be with him when he's
Flying high,
But when things take a turn, you
Leave his side.
Men want you to ride or die.

Give your all or nothing.
And when he needs a helping hand,
Provide something.

That's all men want.

He wants you to only desire him
Despite the fact you are wanted by many men.

He wants to look at you and know that
If he was to lose everything right now,
You would not go,
Because you are loyal.

PS: This is for a man who is worthy of your love.

Hard To Please

Why?
It's like the more I give,
The more you want.

If I give a little,
You want a little more.

If I give you just enough,
It's just not enough.

You want what you want,
And I give you that by any means.

I'm thinking you are happy and
Pleased,
But then you find something else you
Need.

And you never think about me.

All I do is give, give, give.

Do you always have the need to need?
You are so hard to please.

PS: Men don't like to feel this way.

A Lady In The Streets But A Freak For His Needs

A man wants you to be a respectable woman who leaves
A good impression on people.
He wants to feel good when he's with you.

Someone who's charming
And not embarrassing.

Also, when a man needs love,
He needs love.

That's it.
You shouldn't make things so complicated.

If it's extremely early
And he's horny,
Handle it.

Or if it's in the afternoon
And he wants to come inside you,

You should know what to do.
Or if he wants it in the restroom,
Make that move.

Or in the backyard on an empty
Field,
Be prepared for the steel.

Your man wants to get down
And dirty like in the adult movies.

A man wants a lady in the streets
But a freak for his needs.

PS: Be cautious of your surroundings.

Acknowledgments
I would like to thank God and you for your support.

About the Author

Angel Moreira was born in New York City. He attended and graduated from Southwood High School in Shreveport, Louisiana. He has written *Expressions of the Heart* and *The Principles for Loving a Man (What Women Need to Know)* along with R. J. Chaney. In addition, he's written and produced short screenplays, such as *The Transition* and *The Recovery*. Currently he's working on *The Deceit*, *Model Life*, and his first full-length screenplay, *Game's Over*.